OCEAN BREEZES

KNITTED SCARVES inspired by the SEA

Sheryl THIES

Martingale®
& COMPANY

CREDITS

President & CEO ~ Tom Wierzbicki

Publisher ~ Jane Hamada

Editorial Director ~ Mary V. Green

Managing Editor ~ Tina Cook

Technical Editor ~ Ursula Reikes

Copy Editor ~ Liz McGehee

Design Director ~ Stan Green

Assistant Design Director ~ Regina Girard

Illustrator ~ Robin Strobel

Cover & Text Designer ~ Shelly Garrison

Photographer ~ Brent Kane

Ocean Breezes: Knitted Scarves
Inspired by the Sea
© 2007 by Sheryl Thies

Martingale®
& COMPANY

Martingale & Company®
20205 144th Ave. NE
Woodinville, WA 98072-8478 USA
www.martingale-pub.com

Printed in China
12 11 10 09 08 07   8 7 6 5 4 3 2 1

Library of Congress Cataloging-in-Publication Data
Library of Congress Control Number: 2007018867

ISBN: 978-1-56477-801-7

MISSION STATEMENT
Dedicated to providing quality products and service to inspire creativity.

DEDICATION

To Wyatt and Jonah, who shared their knowledge of sea creatures.

ACKNOWLEDGMENTS

Many thanks to all of my knitting friends, especially Melissa, who is a constant source of inspiration; Jacqueline and Ellie, who are talented team knitters; and Ellen, who is a gifted knitter and serves fine wine.

I extend my thanks to Martingale & Company for giving me this opportunity to publish and to all the talented staff who helped with this book. A special thanks to my technical editor, Ursula Reikes, a woman with patience and persistence.

A special thank-you to Wool in the Woods, Knit One Crochet Too, and Rowan yarn companies, who generously provided yarn.

And last but not least, a final thank-you to my family: Kevin, Amos, and Ursula for sharing my enthusiasm and joy.

CONTENTS

Preface ~ 6

Introduction ~ 7

Testing the Waters: Getting Started ~ 8

Projects

    Adriatic Sea ~ 10

    Cockleshell Lace ~ 12

    Coral Branches ~ 14

    Crest o' the Wave ~ 17

    Deep Sea Fishing ~ 20

    Fish Net ~ 24

    Fish Scales ~ 26

    Fishbone Lace ~ 28

    Fisherman's Rib ~ 30

    Goldfish Tails ~ 32

    Green Sea Turtles ~ 35

    Gulls over the Bay ~ 38

Nautical Twisted Rope ~ 41

Kelp Forest ~ 44

Lobster Claws in the Sand ~ 46

Mermaid Mesh ~ 48

Ocean Currents ~ 50

Scallop Shells ~ 52

Sea Cucumbers ~ 54

Sea Foam ~ 56

Sea Horses ~ 58

Snails ~ 61

Starfish on the Beach ~ 64

Surf's Up ~ 67

Turtle Tracks ~ 70

Abbreviations and Glossary ~ 73

Techniques ~ 74

Resources ~ 77

PREFACE

The idea for this collection of scarves began one sunny but windy spring day while walking through the park near my house. Since it was early spring in Wisconsin, the wind chill left me wishing for a scarf. I didn't want to cut my walk short or go back to get a scarf, so I turned up my coat collar and decided to play a mind game where I would think of warm things. Thoughts of summer vacations at the beach brought back the warmest memories. As a kid growing up in the mountains of Pennsylvania, I took numerous trips with my family to Rehoboth Beach in Delaware. As an adult, I visited my brother in Greece, where we would take evening swims in the sea and sail to various islands, sometimes in modest fishing boats. I reflected on jellyfish and seaweed floating in the sea. I reminisced on finding interesting shells and starfish on the beach. I recalled salmon fishing and inadvertently hooking a shark.

As I was nearing home, I thought about trying to knit some of these memories. Later that day, I picked up Barbara Walker's *Treasury of Knitting Patterns* and was amazed to find so many stitch patterns that replicated my memories. I started playing with some of the stitch patterns and realized there were a lot of scarves to be knit.

As spring moved into summer, I had another revelation that inspired more scarves. Wyatt and Jonah, my two grandsons, were swimming in the plastic pool on the deck while I sat by knitting. They started putting on shows, demonstrating dangerous sea creatures and telling me all they knew about the sea. They made lots of waves, some that reached tsunami proportions. And they told me a few fish stories.

The final source of inspiration was my husband. As a diver, he felt it was his duty to weigh in on each scarf. His critiques meant some ideas were scrapped, others reworked, and at times, a quick Internet search was necessary to resolve our differences. He became the final arbiter and deemed each scarf in this collection as being seaworthy.

My hope is that you enjoy making your scarves as much as I enjoyed creating them!

INTRODUCTION

The oceans and seas on our planet are deep and puzzling. Underwater life is full of strange plants and amazing creatures. Often we learn about these mysterious living things only after they wash up on shore. *Ocean Breezes* provides a knitter's view of the curious world of the sea.

The sea has inspired writers, poets, and storytellers throughout the ages. Let the sea inspire your next knitting project. Do you prefer exploring the ocean's depths, with dangerous sharks, sea horses concealed among the coral, or a kelp forest? Do you prefer the legend of the mermaids? Do you like the thrill of surfing and riding that perfect wave all the way to the shore? Or are you the beachcomber who collects the shells and starfish and protects the turtles who trudge ashore to lay their eggs? Or do you prefer fish, either in the wild or in a bowl? Whatever your aquatic connection, *Ocean Breezes* will hold your interest.

These scarves are not just for draping over your shoulders. Wear them wrapped around your neck multiple times, wear them tied around your waist, or lace the sides together and wear as a poncho. Be daring and decorate your surroundings; use them as wall hangings and table runners.

This book has all the information needed to create your interpretation of the sea and the creatures that live there. You will be thrilled with your creations. Read through the information provided to acquaint you with the techniques used. In other words, test the waters before jumping in.

Testing the Waters:
GETTING STARTED

This is a book about texture and patterns. Each project has a unique stitch pattern that is sea related. The techniques include cables, lace, simple yarn-over patterns, twist and crossover stitches, and fancy ribs. There is some complexity with each pattern stitch, but often the pattern is repetitive and the repeat is easily learned. The Craft Yarn Council of America has developed guidelines for determining skill levels. All of the projects fall within two categories, easy and intermediate. Since the finished projects are simple shapes with no shaping, minimal finishing, and a relatively small number of stitches to work with in a row, the actual skill level is not specified for the individual project. If you know how to cast on, knit and purl, bind off, and are drawn to the project, give it a try.

A visit to the local yarn store to select your perfect yarn is a good way to start. You can impose your personal likes and dislikes by selecting your favorite color. You may want to opt for a different fiber content or for a totally different yarn. The choice is yours.

Reading the yarn label will provide guidance when substituting yarn. The label will state the needle size and gauge, fiber content, and care instructions. When substituting yarn, pick a yarn that is a similar thickness. To make this selection easier, there are universal symbols indicating yarn weights (thickness). The weight of the yarn used for each project is indicated with a corresponding symbol. Comparing the yarn-weight symbol to the Standard Yarn-Weight System

STANDARD YARN-WEIGHT SYSTEM						
Yarn-Weight Symbol and Category Names	Super Fine (1)	Fine (2)	Light (3)	Medium (4)	Bulky (5)	Super Bulky (6)
Types of Yarns in Category	Sock, Fingering, Baby	Sport, Baby	DK, Light Worsted	Worsted, Afghan, Aran	Chunky, Craft, Rug	Bulky, Roving
Knit Gauge Ranges in Stockinette Stitch to 4"	27 to 32 sts	23 to 26 sts	21 to 24 sts	16 to 20 sts	12 to 15 sts	6 to 11 sts
Recommended Needle in U.S. Size Range	1 to 3	3 to 5	5 to 7	7 to 9	9 to 11	11 and larger
Recommended Needle in Metric Size Range	2.25 to 3.25 mm	3.25 to 3.75 mm	3.75 to 4.5 mm	4.5 to 5.5 mm	5.5 to 8 mm	8 mm and larger

chart will identify the type of yarn you should be looking for.

Be sure to purchase the correct amount of yarn. Multiply the suggested number of skeins times the amount of yarn on each skein to determine the total number of yards required. This information is listed for each project under materials. Divide the total number of yards required by the amount in each skein of the substituted yarn to determine the number of skeins to purchase.

Any substitution ultimately comes down to gauge. The gauge given for each project may not correspond to the gauge suggested on the yarn-weight chart. The stitch pattern greatly affects the number of stitches per inch. The only way to know if you have the right combination of yarn and needles is to make a gauge swatch.

The gauge swatch is the perfect way to become familiar with the stitch pattern. To make a gauge swatch in a pattern stitch, you want to end up with a knit piece about 4" square. The gauge given as part of the instructions will indicate the number of stitches for 4", but check the pattern-stitch multiple number. If the multiple is 9 plus 4, cast on 22 stitches (9 x 2 repeats + 4 = 22). This will allow you to work two complete pattern repeats. Work in pattern until the piece measures 4". Measure the width of the swatch and divide by 22 stitches for the number of stitches per inch. If the number of stitches per

inch is less than the desired number, go down a needle size and repeat the pattern. If the number of stitches per inch is more than the desired number, go up a needle size.

All gauges for the projects are given after blocking. Stitch patterns before blocking will bunch together and not show the beauty of the stitch. Blocking will open up, spread, and even the stitches out, so you can measure the finished piece to see if it has the proper dimensions. It is amazing how different a blocked piece of lace looks compared to the unblocked piece. Several different methods for blocking are discussed on page 76, and each project has a suggested blocking method.

You may have to swatch and block several times to get to the stated stitch gauge. But don't feel that this is a waste of time. If you want the project to turn out as described, you need to achieve the proper gauge. If you want to freestyle and try something different, go for it. You may end up with a greatly enhanced and desirable piece of work; however, if it doesn't look like the photo, gauge is probably the culprit.

The good news with gauge is that you don't have to deal with row gauge for these scarves. Since all of the patterns are written in inches, rather than rows per inch, row gauge is not even specified in the patterns.

Before going on to the actual project, you may want to work a few more

pattern repeats to become more familiar with the techniques used in the pattern stitch. Some of the stitches and techniques may be new to you, so take a few moments and become familiar with them.

As with most things in life, there are numerous ways of doing things; the same is true with knitting. As with life and knitting, there are subtle differences in the results, depending on how things are done. The stitch patterns are prescriptive, stating a specific way to increase or decrease. If you are not familiar with a term or the exact way of executing the step, refer to the instructions at the end of the book. This will ensure the desired outcome. An "ssk" and a "K2tog" are two ways of decreasing one stitch; however, there is a difference in the slant of the stitch. The "ssk" results in a left-slanting stitch, while the "K2tog" results in a right-slanting stitch. When you are working a pattern stitch, this subtle slant makes a difference.

Several projects have a crochet edge rather than a knit edge. Crochet trims provide a decorative finish and stabilize the edges. Even for a novice, crochet trims can be completed easily and quickly. Instruction for the basics—chain and single crochet—are described on page 75. If you feel you need to practice a crochet stitch, use your gauge swatch and finish it with the crocheted edge.

Adriatic SEA

The Adriatic Sea, an arm of the Mediterranean Sea, is known for its gentle waves and deep blue water. The reversible cable pattern, gently rolled edges, and matte and shine of the ribbon yarn in this scarf aptly reflect the many splendors of the Adriatic Sea.

FINISHED MEASUREMENTS

Approx 6" x 58" (without fringe)

MATERIALS

3 skeins of Zen from Berroco (55% cotton, 45% nylon; 50 g/1.75 oz; 102 m/110 yds), color 8259 [4]

Size 10 needles or size required to obtain gauge

Size 9 needles

Cable needle

Size H-8 (5mm) crochet hook

GAUGE

18 sts = 4" in wave cable patt

WAVE CABLE PATTERN

(Multiple of 6 + 3)

Row 1 (WS): K3, *P3, K3, rep from *.

Rows 2 and 4 (RS): P3, *K3, P3, rep from *.

Rows 3 and 5: Rep row 1.

Row 6: *Sl 3 to cn and hold at back, K3, P3 from cn, rep from * to last 3 sts, K3.

Rows 7, 9, and 11: Rep row 2.

Rows 8 and 10: Rep row 1.

Row 12: P3, *sl 3 to cn and hold at back, K3, P3 from cn, rep from *.

Rep rows 1–12 for patt.

SCARF

With size 9 needles, CO 261 sts. Knit 1 row. Purl 1 row. Knit 1 row.

Change to size 10 needles and work in wave cable patt until piece measures 5½" wide, ending with row 5.

Change to size 9 needles. Knit 1 row. Purl 1 row. Knit 1 row.

With size 10 needles, loosely BO all sts purlwise.

FINISHING

Weave in ends.

Fringe: Cut 34 strands, 15" long. Fold in half and using crochet hook, attach 17 single strands across each narrow edge (page 74).

Block, using the damp-towel method (page 76), to smooth and even sts.

58" without fringe

6"

Cockleshell LACE

The exquisite simplicity of a cockleshell is replicated in this easy-to-work lace pattern. This uncomplicated lace pattern, done in garter stitch, is perfect for the first-time lace knitter, yet has enough variation to hold the interest of an experienced lace knitter.

FINISHED MEASUREMENTS

Approx 6" x 40"

MATERIALS

3 skeins of Douceur et Soie from Knit One Crochet Too (70% baby mohair, 30% silk; 25 g; 205 m/225 yds), color 8100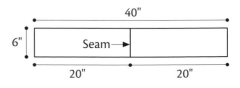

Size 8 needles or size required to obtain gauge

Stitch holder

Tapestry needle

GAUGE

22 sts = 4" in cockleshell lace patt

COCKLESHELL LACE PATTERN

(Patt multiple of 14 +1 plus 4 edge sts)

DD (double decrease): Sl 2 sts tog as if to knit, K1, p2sso.

Row 1 (RS): K2, *K1, YO, K5, DD, K5, YO, rep from * to last 3 sts, K3.

Row 2 and all WS rows: Knit.

Row 3: K2, *K2, YO, K4, DD, K4, YO, K1, rep from * to last 3 sts, K3.

Row 5: K2, *K3, YO, K3, DD, K3, YO, K2, rep from * to last 3 sts, K3.

Row 7: K2, *K4, YO, K2, DD, K2, YO, K3, rep from * to last 3 sts, K3.

Row 9: K2, *K5, YO, K1, DD, K1, YO, K4, rep from * to last 3 sts, K3.

Row 11: K2, *K6, YO, DD, YO, K5, rep from * to last 3 sts, K3.

Row 12: Knit.

Rep rows 1–12 for patt.

SCARF

(Make 2 pieces.)

CO 33 sts and work in cockleshell lace patt until piece measures approx 20", ending with row 12. Move sts to st holder. Make second piece and leave on needle.

FINISHING

Place sts from holder onto knitting needle. Graft 2 pieces tog, using kitchener st (page 74). Weave in ends. Block, using the pin-and-mist method (page 76), to smooth and even sts.

Design Option: For a scarf 11½" wide, purchase a total of 6 skeins of yarn. CO 61 sts and work as directed.

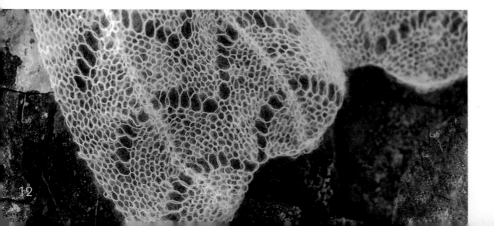

Diagram: rectangle 6" tall × 40" wide, with "Seam →" label and a vertical divider; bottom marked 20" and 20".

CORAL Branches

The variety of shapes and sizes of coral depends on the species; however, this coral branch is a knitter's favorite. The traveling branch can be worked without a cable needle, and the bobble crochet edge is simple to work with only basic crochet skills.

FINISHED MEASUREMENTS

Approx 5½" x 67" (including crochet border)

MATERIALS

4 skeins of Dale of Norway (50% cotton, 40% viscose, 10% silk; 50 g/1.75 oz; 104 m/114 yds), color 3608 (2)

Size 5 needles or size required to obtain gauge

Size F-5 (3.75mm) crochet hook

GAUGE

24 sts = 4" in coral branch patt

CORAL BRANCH PATTERN

(Multiple of 11 + 2)

C2R (cross 2 right): Sk first st on left needle, knit second st, do not sl off, knit skipped st and sl both sts off left needle.

T2R (twist 2 right): Sk first st on left needle, knit second st, do not sl off, purl skipped st and sl both sts off left needle.

MB (make bobble): (K1, YO, K1) into same st, turn, P1, P1 tbl, K1, turn, knit into front and back of next 3 sts; do not turn, pass 5 sts one at a time over last st worked.

C2L (cross 2 left): Sk first st on left needle, knit second st tbl, do not sl off, knit skipped st and sl off left needle.

T2L (twist 2 left): Sk first st on left needle, purl second st tbl, do not sl off, knit skipped st and sl both sts off left needle.

Row 1 (WS): K2, *K4, P1, K6, rep from *.

Row 2 (RS): *P5, C2R, P4, rep from * to last 2 sts, P2.

Row 3: K2, *K4, P2, K5, rep from *.

Row 4: *P4, T2R, K1, P4, rep from * to last 2 sts, P2.

Row 5: K2, *K4, P1, K1, P1, K4, rep from *.

Row 6: *P3, T2R, P1, K1, P4, rep from * to last 2 sts, P2.

Row 7: K2, *K4, P1, K2, P1, K3, rep from *.

Row 8: *P2, T2R, P2, K1, P4, rep from * to last 2 sts, P2.

Row 9: K2, *K4, P1, K3, P1, K2, rep from *.

Row 10: *P2, MB, P3, K1, P4, rep from * to last 2 sts, P2.

Row 11: K2, *K4, P1, K6, rep from *.

Row 12: *P6, C2L, P3, rep from * to last 2 sts, P2.

Row 13: K2, *K3, P2, K6, rep from *.

Row 14: *P6, K1, T2L, P2, rep from * to last 2 sts, P2.

Row 15: K2, *K2, P1, K1, P1, K6, rep from *.

Row 16: *P6, K1, P1, T2L, P1, rep from * to last 2 sts, P2.

Row 17: K2, *K1, P1, K2, P1, K6, rep from *.

Row 18: *P6, K1, P2, T2L, rep from * to last 2 sts, P2.

Row 19: K2, *P1, K3, P1, K6, rep from *.

Row 20: *P6, K1, P3, MB, rep from * to last 2 sts, P2.

Rep rows 1–20 for patt.

SCARF

CO 24 sts and work in coral branch patt until piece measures approx 65", ending with row 1. BO all sts in patt loosely.

FINISHING

With RS facing you and crochet hook, join yarn in second st after any corner, and work 3 rnds of edging as follows:

MB (make bobble): (Yarn around hook, draw up loop) 3 times in next st, draw loop through all 7 loops on hook.

Rnd 1: Sc all around scarf, working 3 sc in each corner; join with slip st, ch 1.

Rnd 2: Work 1 sc in same st as join, *MB, ch 1, sk 1 st, rep from * to 2 sts before corner, MB in each of next 4 sts, cont from * to last sc, sc, join with sl st.

Rnd 3: Sc in each st and on top of each bobble, join with sl st.

Fasten off. Weave in ends. Block, using the mist method (page 76), to smooth and even sts.

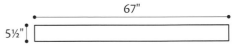

Measurements include crochet border.

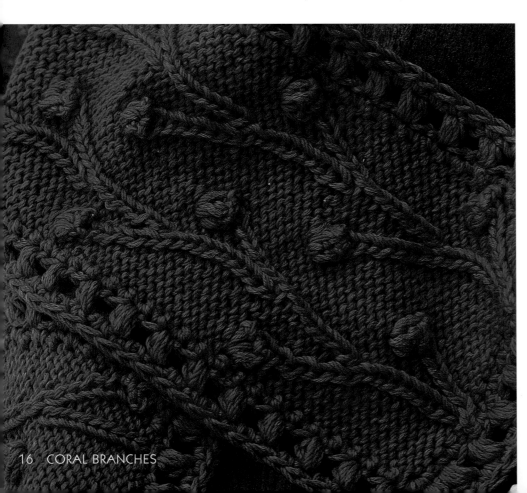

CREST O' THE WAVE

The crest is the highest point of the wave. This delicate lace stitch comes from the Shetland Islands and is easily memorized, making it fairly easy to stitch. Started at the bottom, the triangle is formed by a simple eyelet border that edges the Crest o' the Wave pattern. The silk-ribbon trim is woven into the eyelet border for added embellishment.

FINISHED MEASUREMENTS

Approx 57" along top edge x 27"

MATERIALS

3 skeins of New England Shetland from Harrisville Designs (100% pure wool; 50 g/1.75 oz; 196 yds), color 27 **2**

Size 7 circular (29") needle or size required to obtain gauge

8 yards of 1"-wide Hanah Silk Ribbon from Artemis, color HV hydrangea

GAUGE

17 sts = 4" in Crest o' Wave patt after blocking

BORDER ROW

K2, YO, knit to end.

CREST O' WAVE PATTERN

(Patt multiple of 12 +1 plus 6 edge sts. There is a 1-st inc in every row.)

Row 1 (RS): K2, YO, knit to end.

Rows 2, 3, and 4: Rep row 1.

Row 5: K2, YO, K2, *K2tog twice, (YO, K1) 3 times, YO, ssk twice, K1, rep from * to last 3 sts, K3.

Rows 6, 8, and 10: K2, YO, K1, purl to last 4 sts, K4.

Row 7: K2, YO, K3, *K2tog twice, (YO, K1) 3 times, YO, ssk twice, K1, rep from *to last 4 sts, K4.

Row 9: K2, YO, K4, *K2tog twice, (YO, K1) 3 times, YO, ssk twice, K1, rep from * to last 5 sts, K5.

Row 11: K2, YO, K5, *K2tog twice, (YO, K1) 3 times, YO, ssk twice, K1, rep from * to last 6 sts, K6.

Row 12: K2, YO, K1, purl to last 4 sts, K4.

Rep rows 1–12 for patt.

SCARF

CO 9 sts. Work border row 6 times—15 sts.

Work in Crest o' Wave patt until 18 patt reps have been completed—231 sts.

Work border row 4 times.

Next row: K2, YO, *K2tog, YO, rep from * to last 3 sts, K3.

Work border row once. BO all sts loosely.

FINISHING

Weave in ends. Block, using the wet-blocking method (page 76), to smooth and even sts.

Top ribbon trim: Cut 3 yds of ribbon. With RS facing you, beg at right top edge, *weave ribbon with fingers from WS to RS through eyelet hole, sk 2 holes, and move ribbon to back, rep from * across (see diagram above right). Adjust ribbon so that it rolls over the top edge. Leave ends of ribbon free to dangle as fringe.

Side ribbon trim: Cut 2½ yds of ribbon for each side. With RS facing you, beg at top edge and working toward bottom, weave ribbon as for top ribbon.

Use overhand knot (below) to secure ribbon fringe at side, top, and bottom.

Design Option: This scarf is beautiful by itself and can be worn without the ribbon embellishment.

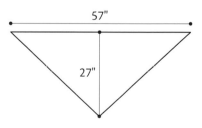

57"

27"

DEEP SEA Fishing

Long lines are required for deep sea fishing, and sometimes a dog shark is snagged. Edged with a shark-fin border, this long scarf includes loads of fishhooks. This is one deep sea fishing expedition that ensures a good catch!

FINISHED MEASUREMENTS

Approx 9" x 95"

MATERIALS

2 skeins of Silk Rhapsody from Art Yarns (100% silk and 70% kid mohair, 30% silk; 100 g; 238 m/260 yds), color 107 (4)

Size 8 needles or size required to obtain gauge

Stitch holder

Tapestry needle

GAUGE

17 sts = 4" in fishhooks patt

SHARK FIN EDGING

Row 1 (WS): Sl 1, K1, (YO, K2tog) twice, YO, K2.

Row 2 (RS): K2, YO, K2, (YO, K2tog) twice, K1.

Row 3: Sl 1, K1, (YO, K2tog) twice, K2, YO, K2.

Row 4: K2, YO, K4, (YO, K2tog) twice, K1.

Row 5: Sl 1, K1, (YO, K2tog) twice, K4, YO, K2.

Row 6: K2, YO, K6, (YO, K2tog) twice, K1.

Row 7: Sl 1, K1, (YO, K2tog) twice, K6, YO, K2.

Row 8: K2, YO, K8, (YO, K2tog) twice, K1.

Row 9: Sl 1, K1, (YO, K2tog) twice, K8, YO, K2.

Row 10: K2, YO, K10, (YO, K2tog) twice, K1.

Row 11: Sl 1, K1, (YO, K2tog) twice, K10, Y0, K2.

Row 12: BO 11 sts, K2, (YO, K2tog,) twice, K1.

Rep rows 1–12 for patt.

FISHHOOKS PATTERN

(Patt multiple of 8 + 1 plus 5 edge sts)

Row 1 and all WS rows: K3, P32, K3.

Rows 2 and 4 (RS): Knit.

Row 6: K9, *ssk, YO, K1, YO, K2tog, K3, rep from * to last 5 sts, K5.

Row 8: K8, *ssk, YO, K3, YO, K2tog, K1, rep from * to last 6 sts, K6.

Row 10: K11, *ssk, YO, K6, rep from * to last 3 sts, K3.

Row 12: K10, *ssk, YO, K6, rep from * to last 4 sts, K4.

Row 14: K9, *ssk, YO, K6, rep from * to last 5 sts, K5.

Row 16: K8, *ssk, YO, K6, rep from * to last 6 sts, K6.

Rows 18 and 20: Knit.

Row 22: K9, *ssk, YO, K1, YO, K2tog, K3, rep from * to last 5 sts, K5.

Row 24: K8, *ssk, YO, K3, YO, K2tog, K1, rep from * to last 6 sts, K6.

Row 26: K10, *YO, K2tog, K6, rep from * to last 4 sts, K4.

Row 28: K11, *YO, K2tog, K6, rep from * to last 3 sts, K3.

Row 30: K12, *YO, K2tog, K6, rep from * to last 2 sts, K2.

Row 32: K7, *K6, YO, K2tog, rep from * to last 7 sts, K7.

Rep rows 1–32 for patt.

SCARF

(Make 2 pieces.)

CO 8 sts and knit 1 row.

Work in Shark Fin edging until piece measures 9", ending with row 12. BO 8 sts and cut yarn.

PU 38 sts along straight edge of Shark Fin edging. Work in fishhooks patt until piece measures approx 47½", ending with row 16 or 32. Work rows 1 and 2 once more.

Place all sts onto st holder.

Make second piece and leave sts on needle.

FINISHING

Place sts from holder onto knitting needle. Graft 2 pieces tog, using kitchener st (page 74).

Weave in ends. Block, using the mist method (page 76), to smooth and even sts.

Design Option: Turn the fishhooks into candy canes by working the fishhooks patt in reverse. Beg with row 32 and work to row 1.

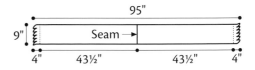

Fish NET

Fish Net can be used in so many ways. Tie on a few shells and use it as a decorative wall hanging. Tie it around your waist as a partial beach cover-up. Or simply drape it around your neck and head as a stylish scarf.

FINISHED MEASUREMENTS

Approx 7" x 78"

MATERIALS

1 skein of Bamboo from South West Trading Company (100% bamboo; 100 g; 250 yds), color 521 Chocolate

Size 8 needles or size required to obtain gauge

Size 10½ needles for bind off

GAUGE

Approx 20 sts = 4" in fish net patt on size 8 needles

FISH NET PATTERN

(Odd number of sts)

Row 1: K1, *YO, sl 1, K1, pass YO and sl st tog over knit st, rep from *.

Row 2: P1, *YO, P1, rep from *.

Rep rows 1 and 2 for patt.

SCARF

CO 35 sts and knit 2 rows.

Work in fish net patt until piece measures approx 78", ending with row 2.

Knit 2 rows.

With 10½ needles, BO all sts very loosely.

FINISHING

Weave in ends. Block, using the pin-and-mist method (page 76), to smooth and even sts.

Design Option: To make a wall hanging approximately 20" wide, purchase an additional ball of yarn and CO 100 sts; work to desired length. Tie on shells for additional embellishment.

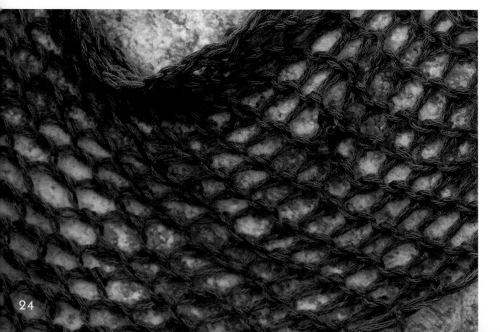

FISH Scales

The primary purpose of scales is to give the fish external protection. However, the primary purpose for these scales is to give this scarf textural interest.

FINISHED MEASUREMENTS

Approx 41" across top edge x 11¼"

MATERIALS

1 skein of hand-dyed Stardust from Judi and Co (55% nylon, 39% wool, 6% poly; 100 yds), color Raspberry Ice

Size 15 needles or size required to obtain gauge

Size 19 needles for bind off

GAUGE

9 sts = 4" in fish scale patt on size 15 needles

FISH SCALE PATTERN

(Odd number of sts)

YO in reverse: Bring yarn over needle from back to front and then between needles to back.

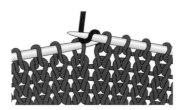

Rows 1 and 3 (WS): (K1f&b) twice, purl to last 2 sts, (K1f&b) twice.

Row 2: K2, *YO in reverse, K2, pass YO over 2 knit sts, rep from * to last st, K1.

Row 4: K1, *YO in reverse, K2, pass YO over 2 knit sts, rep from * to last 2 sts, K2.

Rep rows 1–4 for patt.

SCARF

With size 15 needles, CO 9 sts and work in fish scale patt until 93 sts are on needle, ending with RS row.

With size 19 needles, BO all sts in patt loosely.

FINISHING

Weave in ends. Block, using the mist method (page 76), to smooth and even sts.

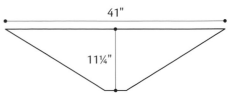

FISHBONE Lace

Worked in the round, this fishbone lace pattern requires no purling. Qiviut (pronounced ki-vee-ute) is the Arctic musk ox's downy-soft underwool, which is combed rather than sheared. Qiviut is not scratchy and will not shrink, making it the perfect fiber for a cowl.

FINISHED MEASUREMENTS

Approx 20½" circumference x 12¼" long

MATERIALS

1 skein of Qiviut from Cricket Cove (100% qiviut; 2 oz; 187 yds), color Natural 〔3〕

Size 8 circular (16") needle or size required to obtain gauge

Stitch marker

GAUGE

19 sts = 4" in fishbone lace patt

FISHBONE LACE PATTERN

(Multiple of 7 sts, worked in the round)

Rnd 1: *K4, YO, sl 1, K2tog, psso, YO, rep from *.

Rnd 2: Knit.

Rep rows 1 and 2 for patt.

COWL

CO 98 sts. Join sts, being careful not to twist them, and pm for beg of rnd.

Knit 2 rnds.

Beg fishbone lace patt and work until piece measures 12", ending with rnd 2.

Knit 1 rnd.

BO all sts loosely.

Remember not to get the yarn twisted. After casting on, do not turn work. Check work carefully to make sure the cast-on stitches are not twisted around the needle. Knit into the first cast-on stitch to join. Check your work again after several rows. If a twist is found, you'll have to start over.

FINISHING

Weave in ends. Block, using the mist method (page 76), to smooth and even sts.

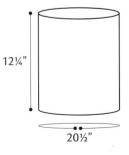

12¼"

20½"

Fisherman's RIB

This deeply textured ribbing takes on a more feminine appearance with the dropped-stitch-loop edge. Fish beads add the final touch of embellishment.

FINISHED MEASUREMENTS

Approx 3½" x 51" (without loop edge)

MATERIALS

2 skeins of KPPPM from Koigu (100% merino wool; 50 g; 160 m/175 yds), color 212 **2**

Size 7 needles or size required to obtain gauge

8 fish beads

16 beads (4 mm)

Clear fingernail polish

GAUGE

25 sts = 4" in fisherman's rib patt

FISHERMAN'S RIB PATTERN

(Even number of sts)

All rows: *P1, knit next st in row below (page 74), rep from * to last 2 sts, P2.

SCARF

CO 24 sts and purl 1 row.

Work in fisherman's rib patt until piece measures approx 51".

Work in patt to last st, slide rem st off left needle. Turn and BO in patt until 1 st rem on left needle. Fasten off st on right needle. Slide rem st off left needle. Carefully unravel dropped-edge st, creating loops. Knot 2 loops tog and tighten knot next to worked sts. Cont unraveling and knotting to CO edge. Rep on other side.

FINISHING

Weave in ends. Do not block ribbing; lightly mist edge loops, if necessary, to smooth.

Embellishment: Cut 6" strand of yarn and knot at one end. String purchased bead onto yarn, string fish bead, string 3 beads, string fish bead. Fasten to corner by weaving strand into knitted work. Rep for each corner. To secure knot, place a dab of clear fingernail polish on knot and allow to dry.

Design Option:

For a more masculine scarf, purchase 4 skeins in a more manly colorway. CO 36 sts and work to desired length. BO all sts rather than dropping edge sts for loops.

51" not including loop edge

3½"

Generally, when working with hand-dyed yarns, it is advisable to work from two balls, alternating two rows from one ball and two rows from the second ball while carrying the yarns up the side. However, on this scarf, carrying the alternate yarns up the side would interfere with the dropped-stitch-loop edge, so you need to work from only one ball at a time.

GOLDFISH Tails

The fish-tail lace pattern is as mesmerizing as watching goldfish in an aquarium. The bobble trim accentuates and outlines the fish tails, and the L shape means this scarf will stay on.

FINISHED MEASUREMENTS

Approx 39" x 39" (along outside edges of L shape)

MATERIALS

4 skeins of Cherub from Wool in the Woods (100% merino wool; 200 yds), color Buttercup (2)

Size 10 needles or size required to obtain gauge

Tapestry needle

GAUGE

17 sts = 4" in fish-tail lace patt

BOTTOM BOBBLE EDGE

(Multiple of 6 + 5)

MB (make bobble): (K1f&b twice, K1) in same st, turn, K5, turn, P5, turn, K5, turn; sl 2nd, 3rd, 4th, and 5th st over first st, K1.

Row 1 (WS): Knit.

Row 2 (RS): K2, *MB, K5, rep from * to last 3 sts, MB, K2.

Row 3: Knit.

FISH-TAIL LACE PATTERN WITH BOBBLE-EDGE SIDES

(Patt multiple of 8 + 1 plus 10 sts for bobble-edge sides)

Row 1 (RS): K6, *YO, K2, sl 1, K2tog, psso, K2, YO, K1, rep from * to last 5 sts, K5.

Row 2 and all WS rows: K5, purl to last 5 sts, K5.

Row 3: K2, MB, K4, *YO, K1, sl 1, K2tog, psso, K1, YO, K3, rep from * to last 12 sts, YO, K1, sl 1, K2tog, psso, K1, YO, K4, MB, K2.

Row 5: K8, *YO, sl 1, K2tog, psso, YO, K5, rep from * to last 11 sts, YO, sl 1, K2tog, psso, YO, K8.

Row 6: K5, purl to last 5 sts, K5.

Rep rows 1–6 for patt.

Work from two balls of hand-dyed yarn at the same time to achieve an even color effect. Work two rows from one ball, then two rows from second ball. Do not cut yarn; instead, carry yarn up side of work.

PIECE A

CO 65 sts and work rows 1–3 of Bottom Bobble edge, inc 2 sts evenly across last row—67 sts.

Work in fish-tail lace patt until piece measures approx 39", slightly stretched, ending with row 6.

Knit 1 row and dec 2 sts evenly across row—65 sts.

Work rows 1–3 of Bottom Bobble edge. BO all sts loosely.

PIECE B

Work as for piece A until piece measures approx 24", slightly stretched, ending with row 6.

Knit 2 rows.

BO all sts loosely.

FINISHING

With RS facing you, sew BO edge of B to side edge of A as shown (see diagram at right). Weave in all ends. Block, using the pin-and-mist method (page 76), to smooth and even sts.

Design Option: For a more subdued look, you can eliminate the bobbles along the side edges of the fish-tail lace patt by working a knit st in place of MB.

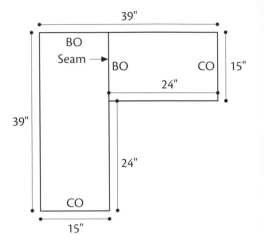

GREEN Sea Turtles

The green sea turtle's bony outer shell is streamlined and light. Using their flippers, these animals are swift and graceful swimmers. This scarf, tipped with ribbed cuffs, uses a cable pattern to form the turtle shell and flippers. The sides have a crocheted shell edge. The back side of the cable pattern forms an attractive structural fabric, which could be used as the right side, making this a reversible scarf.

FINISHED MEASUREMENTS

Approx 14" x 69" (including crochet shell edging)

MATERIALS

5 skeins of Ultra Alpaca from Berroco (50% alpaca, 50% wool; 100 g/3.5 oz; 198 m/215 yds), color 6251

Size 10 needles or size required to obtain gauge

Cable needle

Size J-10 (6 mm) crochet hook

Decorative shawl pin (optional)

GAUGE

22 sts = 4" in turtle check patt, slightly stretched

TURTLE CHECK PATTERN

(Multiple of 12 + 2)

T4LF (twist 4 left front): Sl 1 to cn and hold at front, P3, K1 from cn.

T4RB (twist 4 right back): Sl 3 to cn and hold at back, K1, P3 from cn.

Row 1 (RS): K4, P6, *K6, P6, rep from * to last 4 sts, K4.

Row 2: P4, K6, *P6, K6, rep from * to last 4 sts, P4.

Row 3: K3, T4LF, T4RB, *K4, T4LF, T4RB, rep from * to last 3 sts, K3.

Row 4: P3, K3, P2, K3, *P4, K3, P2, K3, rep from * to last 3 sts, P3.

Row 5: K2, *T4LF, K2, T4RB, K2, rep from *.

Row 6: P2, *K3, P4, K3, P2, rep from *.

Row 7: K1, *T4LF, K4, T4RB, rep from * to last st, K1.

Rows 8–11: Rep rows 1 and 2 twice.

Row 12: Rep row 1.

Row 13: K1, *T4RB, K4, T4LF, rep from * to last st, K1.

Row 14: Rep row 6.

Row 15: K2, *T4RB, K2, T4LF, K2, rep from *.

Row 16: Rep row 4.

Row 17: K3, T4RB, T4LF, *K4, T4RB, T4LF, rep from * to last 3 sts, K3.

Row 18: Rep row 2.

Rows 19 and 20: Rep rows 1 and 2.

Rep rows 1–20 for patt.

SCARF

CO 74 sts and work in K1, P1 ribbing until piece measures 4". Knit 1 row, purl 1 row.

Work turtle check patt until piece measures approx 65", ending with row 10 or 20.

Knit 1 row, purl 1 row.

Work in K1, P1 ribbing for 4".

BO all sts in patt loosely.

CROCHET SHELL EDGE

On one long edge, with RS facing you, work shell edging as follows:

Row 1: Join yarn in first st above ribbing, work 1 row of sc (see page 75) to end of Turtle Check patt at opposite end. Fasten off.

Row 2: Do not turn. With RS facing you, go back to beg of sc row and rejoin yarn in last st of ribbing. Work

shells from right to left as follows: (sc, ch 3, work 3 dc) in joining st, sk 2 sts, *(sc, ch 3, work 3 dc) in next st, sk 2 sts, rep from * across. Work last shell just after last sc by working (sc, ch 3, 3 dc) in first st of ribbing. Fasten off.

Rep rows 1 and 2 on opposite long edge.

FINISHING

Weave in ends. Block, using the pin-and-mist method (page 76), to smooth and even sts.

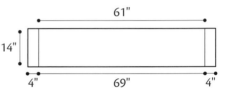

Measurements include crochet shell edging.

Wrong side of turtle check pattern

Gulls OVER THE Bay

Your imaginary trip to the beach is complete with gentle waves lapping at the water's edge and gulls circling overhead. Wear this garment as a poncho laced together with silk ribbon, or as a wrap without the ribbon. Either way, this gorgeous piece won't migrate to the back of your closet but will remain a favorite, season after season.

FINISHED MEASUREMENTS

Approx 14" x 74"

MATERIALS

2 skeins of Cotton Woven Ribbon from Blue Heron Yarns (100% cotton; 400 yds), color Deep Blue Sea 5

Size 11 circular (29") needle or size required to obtain gauge

5 yds of 1½"-wide Hanah Silk Ribbon from Artemis, color SG Sea Goddess

Size K-10½ (6.5 mm) crochet hook

Optional: 36 stitch markers

GAUGE

14 sts = 4" in gull wings patt

WAVE EDGE PATTERN

(Worked over 13 sts)

Row 1 and all WS rows: K2, purl to last 2 sts, K2.

Row 2 (RS): Sl 1, K3, YO, K5, YO, K2tog, YO, K2—15 sts.

Row 4: Sl 1, K4, sl 1, K2tog, psso, K2, (YO, K2tog) twice, K1—13 sts.

Row 6: Sl 1, K3, ssk, K2, (YO, K2tog), twice, K1—12 sts.

Row 8: Sl 1, K2, ssk, K2, (YO, K2tog) twice, K1—11 sts.

Row 10: Sl 1, K1, ssk, K2, (YO, K2tog) twice, K1—10 sts.

Row 12: K1, ssk, K2, YO, K1, YO, K2tog, YO, K2—11 sts.

Row 14: Sl 1, (K3, YO) twice, K2tog, YO, K2—13 sts.

Rep rows 1–14 for patt.

GULL WINGS PATTERN

(Multiple of 7 sts)

Row 1 and all WS rows: Purl.

Row 2 (RS): *K1, K2tog, YO, K1, YO, ssk, K1, rep from *.

Row 4: *K2tog, YO, K3, YO, ssk, rep from *.

Row 6: Knit.

Rep rows 1–6 for patt.

SCARF

CO 13 sts and work wave edge patt until piece measures approx 74", slightly stretched, ending with row 14. BO all sts loosely.

With RS of edge piece facing you, PU 259 sts along straight edge. Work gull wings patt a total of 9 reps, ending with row 6.

Purl 1 row. Knit 1 row. Purl 1 row. Loosely BO all sts knitwise.

When beginning gull wings pattern, you can use stitch markers to indicate pattern repeats. If desired, place marker every seven stitches to indicate pattern repeat.

Note: To achieve an even color effect, alternate between two skeins of hand-dyed yarn by working two rows from one ball, then two rows from the second ball. Carry alternate yarns up the side.

FINISHING

Edging: Beg at bottom right-hand corner with RS facing you and size K crochet hook. Work 1 row of sc (page 75) up narrow end of scarf, across top edge, and down rem narrow end. Cut yarn. Join yarn at top left-hand corner and work 1 row of crab st (page 75) along top edge only.

Weave in all ends. Block, using the pin-and-mist method (page 76), to smooth and even sts.

Ribbon lacing for poncho: Fold piece in half lengthwise, holding the 2 shorter edges tog. Measure 14" from center fold and mark with safety pin. Count an even number of eyelet openings from bottom edge to marker; adjust safety pin, if necessary, to get an even number of openings. Fold ribbon in half; working on RS and beg at marker, lace the ribbon, using the straight-lacing method at right . Allow extra ribbon to hang at bottom edge.

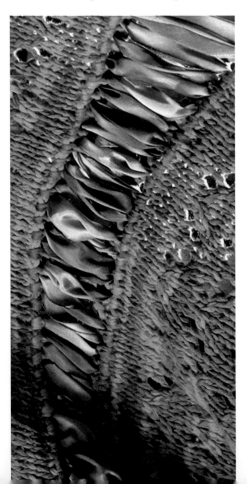

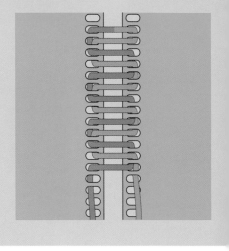

Straight Lacing

*Start each end of the ribbon from the wrong side and feed it up through an eyelet to the right side, across the gap, down through the eyelet to the wrong side. Skip one eyelet on the same side and repeat from *.

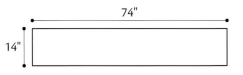

Design Option: This garment can be worn simply as a rectangular wrap rather than as a ribbon-laced poncho.

74"

14"

Nautical TWISTED Rope

Walk along the docks and you'll see the coils of bulky weathered rope. This scarf conveys the old sea touch that any sailor will admire. The bold cable pattern appears complex but works up quickly.

FINISHED MEASUREMENTS

Approx 8" x 56"

MATERIALS

2 skeins of Cascade 220 from Cascade Yarns (100% Peruvian Highland wool; 100 g/3.5 oz; 220 yds), color 8013

4

Size 8 needles or size required to obtain gauge

Cable needle

GAUGE

24 sts = 4" in nautical cable patt, slightly stretched

NAUTICAL CABLE PATTERN

(Worked over 49 sts)

Front cross (FC): Sl 2 sts to cn and hold at front, K2, K2 from cn.

Back cross (BC): Sl 2 sts to cn and hold at back, K2, K2 from cn.

Row 1 (RS): (P2, K4) 4 times, P1, (K4, P2) 4 times.

Rows 2, 4, 6, and 8: (K2, P4) 4 times, K1, (P4, K2) 4 times.

Row 3: (P2, FC, P2, K4) twice, P1, (K4, P2, BC, P2) twice.

Row 5: (P2, K4) 4 times, P1, (K4, P2) 4 times.

Row 7: P2, FC, P2, K4, P2, FC, P2, sl 5 sts to cn and hold at front, K4, sl purl st from cn to left needle and purl it, K4 from cn, P2, BC, P2, K4, P2, BC, P2.

Row 9: P2, K4, P2, M1, (K4, P2) twice, K4, M1, P1, M1, (K4, P2) twice, K4, M1, P2, K4, P2—53 sts.

Row 10: K2, P4, *K3, P4, (K2, P4) twice, rep from * once, K3, P4, K2.

Row 11: P2, FC, P3, M1, K4, P2tog, FC, P2tog, K4, M1, P3, M1, K4, P2tog, BC, P2tog, K4, M1, P3, BC, P2.

Row 12: K2, P4, K4, (P4, K1) twice, P4, K5, (P4, K1) twice, P4, K4, P4, K2.

Row 13: P2, K4, P4, M1, K3, ssk, K4, K2tog, K3, M1, P5, M1, K3, ssk, K4, K2tog, K3, M1, P4, K4, P2.

Row 14: K2, P4, K5, P12, K7, P12, K5, P4, K2.

Row 15: P2, FC, P5, M1, K4, FC, K4, M1, P7, M1, K4, BC, K4, M1, P5, BC, P2—57 sts.

Row 16: K2, P4, K6, P12, K9, P12, K6, P4, K2.

Row 17: P2, K4, P6, sl 8 sts to cn and hold at back, K4, sl second 4 sts from cn to left needle and knit them, K4 from cn, P9, sl 8 sts to cn and hold at front, K4, sl second 4 sts from cn to left needle and knit them, K4 from cn, P6, K4, P2.

Row 18: K2, P4, K6, P12, K9, P12, K6, P4, K2.

Row 19: P2, FC, P4, P2tog, K4, FC, K4, P2tog, P5, P2tog, K4, BC, K4, P2tog, P4, BC, P2— 53 sts.

Row 20: K2, P4, K5, P12, K7, P12, K5, P4, K2.

Row 21: P2, K4, P3, *P2tog, (K4, M1) twice, K4, P2tog, P3, rep from * once, K4, P2.

Row 22: K2, P4, K4, (P4, K1) twice, P4, K5, (P4, K1) twice, P4, K4, P4, K2.

Row 23: P2, FC, P2, P2tog, K4, M1, P1, FC, P1, M1, K4, P2tog, P1, P2tog, K4, M1, P1, BC, P1, M1, K4, P2tog, P2, BC, P2.

Row 24: K2, P4, *K3, P4, (K2, P4) twice, rep from * once, K3, P4, K2.

Row 25: P2, K4, P1, P2tog, (K4, P2) twice, K4, P3tog, (K4, P2) twice, K4, P2tog, P1, K4, P2— 49 sts.

Row 26: (K2, P4) 4 times, K1, (P4, K2) 4 times.

Row 27: P2, FC, P2, K4, P2, FC, P2, sl 5 sts to cn and hold at front, K4, sl purl st from cn to left needle and purl it, K4 from cn, P2, BC, P2, K4, P2, BC, P2.

Row 28: (K2, P4) 4 times, K1, (P4, K2) 4 times.

Rep rows 1–28 for patt.

SCARF

CO 49 sts and work in nautical cable patt until piece measures approx 56", ending with row 2.

BO all sts in patt loosely.

FINISHING

Weave in ends. Block, using the mist method (page 76), to smooth and even sts.

KELP Forest

Kelp is more than just the seaweeds that float in the ocean and wash up on the beach. Kelp forests provide habitat for sea creatures and even help reduce the chop from the afternoon winds that surfers complain about. The fancy rib seaweed pattern makes a nice scarf for men and women, boys and girls.

FINISHED MEASUREMENTS

Approx 5" x 55"

MATERIALS

3 skeins of Premiere from Classic Elite Yarns (50% pima cotton, 50% tencel; 50 g; 108 yds), color 5297 Wood Fern

3

Size 6 needles or size required to obtain gauge

Stitch holder

Tapestry needle

GAUGE

28 sts = 4" in seaweed st patt, slightly stretched

SEAWEED STITCH PATTERN

(Multiple of 6)

Row 1 (WS): *P4, K2, rep from *.

Row 2 and all RS rows: Knit the knit sts and purl the purl sts as they face you.

Row 3: *P3, K3, rep from *.

Row 5: *P2, K4, rep from *.

Row 7: P1, *K4, P2, rep from * to last 5 sts, K4, P1.

Row 9: P1, *K3, P3, rep from * to last 5 sts, K3, P2.

Row 11: P1, *K2, P4, rep from * to last 5 sts, K2, P3.

Row 12: Knit the knit sts and purl the purl sts as they face you.

Rep rows 1–12 for patt.

SCARF

(Make 2 pieces)

CO 36 sts. Work in seaweed st patt until piece measures approx 27½", ending with row 12.

Purl 1 row. Place all sts on st holder.

Make second piece and leave sts on needles.

FINISHING

Place sts from holder onto knitting needle. Graft 2 pieces tog, using kitchener st (page 74). Weave in ends. Block, using the mist method (page 76), to smooth and even sts.

Design Option: For an 8"-wide scarf, CO 48 sts and work as directed to desired length. You'll need 2 additional skeins of yarn.

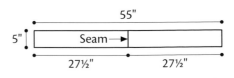

Lobster Claws IN THE SAND

The lobster defends itself with its large pincher claws. Imbedded in the sandy texture of this scarf, these claws will not pinch and are for ornamental purposes only. If you dare, you can use this scarf as a table runner at your next lobster boil!

FINISHED MEASUREMENTS

Approx 5½" x 56½"

MATERIALS

2 skeins of Classic Silk from Classic Elite Yarns (50% cotton, 30% silk, 20% nylon; 50 g; 135 yds), color 6955 Tomato (3)

Size 7 needles or size required to obtain gauge

Cable needle

GAUGE

20 sts = 4" in lobster claws patt

SAND STITCH PATTERN

(Even number of sts)

Rows 1 and 3 (WS): Knit.

Row 2 (RS): *K1, P1, rep from *.

Row 4: *P1, K1, rep from *.

Rep rows 1–4 for patt.

LOBSTER CLAWS PATTERN

(Worked over 28 sts)

Row 1 (WS): Knit.

Row 2 (RS): (K1, P1) 4 times, P2, K1, P6, K1, P2, (K1, P1) 4 times.

Rows 3, 5, and 7: K10, P2, K4, P2, K10.

Row 4: (P1, K1) 4 times, P2, K2, P4, K2, P2, (P1, K1) 4 times.

Row 6: (K1, P1) 4 times, P2, K2, P4, K2, P2, (K1, P1) 4 times.

Row 8: (P1, K1) 4 times, P2, sl 2 to cn and hold at front, P2, YO, K2tog tbl from cn, sl 2 to cn, hold at back, K2tog tbl, YO, P2 from cn, P2, (P1, K1) 4 times.

Rep rows 1–8 for patt.

SCARF

CO 28 sts. Work 8 rows of sand st patt.

Work lobster claws patt until piece measures approx 55", ending with row 8.

Work 8 rows of sand st patt.

BO all sts in patt loosely.

FINISHING

Weave in ends. Block, using the mist method (page 76), to smooth and even sts.

56½"

5½"

Mermaid MESH

Tales of mermaids are universal and have enticed the human race for centuries. Delight your little mermaid with a scarf stitched in this magical mesh lace pattern.

FINISHED MEASUREMENTS

Approx 5" x 55"

MATERIALS

2 skeins of String of Pearls from Muench (70% cotton, 20% rayon, 10% polyester; 50 g; 99 yds), color 4004 (4)

Size 10½ needles or size required to obtain gauge

GAUGE

17 sts = 4" in mermaid mesh patt, slightly stretched

MERMAID MESH PATTERN

(Multiple of 9 + 4)

Row 1 (WS) and all other odd-numbered rows: Purl, working "YO twice" as K1, P1.

Row 2 (RS): K1, YO, *(ssk, YO) 3 times, K3tog, YO twice, rep from * to last 3 sts, ssk, K1.

Row 4: *K2tog, YO twice, (ssk, YO) twice, K3tog, YO, rep from * to last 4 sts, K2tog, YO, K2.

Row 6: K1, *K2tog, YO twice, ssk, YO, K3tog, YO, K2tog, YO, rep from * to last 3 sts, K2tog, YO, K1.

Row 8: K2tog, YO, *K2tog, YO twice, sl 1, K2tog, psso, (YO, K2tog) twice, YO, rep from * to last 2 sts, K2.

Row 10: K1, K2tog, YO, *K2tog, YO twice, sl 1, K2tog, psso, (YO, K2tog) twice, YO, rep from, * to last st, K1.

Row 12: K2tog, YO, *K2tog, YO twice, ssk, YO, sl 1, K2tog, psso, YO, K2tog, YO, rep from * to last 2 sts, K2.

Row 14: K1, K2tog, *YO twice, (ssk, YO) twice, sl 1, K2tog, psso, YO, K2tog, rep from * to last st, YO, K1.

Row 16: K2tog, *YO twice, (ssk, YO) 3 times, K3tog, rep from * to last 2 sts, YO twice, ssk.

Rep rows 1–16 for patt.

SCARF

CO 22 sts and work in mermaid mesh patt until piece measures approx 55", ending with row 1.

Loosely BO all sts purlwise.

FINISHING

Weave in ends. Block, using the damp-towel method (page 76), to smooth and even sts.

Design Options: Wear this garment as a sash wrapped around your waist. Or, for a 15"-wide scarf, CO 66 sts and work as directed. You'll need 6 skeins of yarn for this wider version.

OCEAN Currents

Complex ocean currents are created by the constant movement of the water. This attractive stitch pattern conveys the graceful motion of water, while the soft shimmer of the silk yarn calls to mind the glistening surface of the ocean.

FINISHED MEASUREMENTS

Approx 6" x 50"

MATERIALS

2 skeins of Regal Silk from Art Yarns (100% silk; 50 g; 163 yds), color 115

Size 6 needles or size required to obtain gauge

GAUGE

30 sts = 4" in ocean current pattern

OCEAN CURRENT PATTERN

(Patt worked over 37 sts plus 8 edge sts)

Row 1 (RS): K4, YO, K10, K2tog tbl, K9, K2tog, K9, YO, K5, K4.

Row 2: K4, P6, YO, P9, P2tog, P7, P2tog tbl, P10, YO, P1, K4.

Row 3: K4, K2, YO, K10, K2tog tbl, K5, K2tog, K9, YO, K7, K4.

Row 4: K4, P8, YO, P9, P2tog, P3, P2tog tbl, P10, YO, P3, K4.

Row 5: K4, K4, YO, K10, K2tog tbl, K1, K2tog, K9, YO, K9, K4.

Row 6: K4, YO, P9, P2tog, P9, P2tog tbl, P10, YO, P5, K4.

Row 7: K4, K6, YO, K10, K2tog tbl, K7, K2tog, K9, YO, K1, K4.

Row 8: K4, P2, YO, P9, P2tog, P5, P2tog tbl, P10, YO, P7, K4.

Row 9: K4, K8, YO, K10, K2tog tbl, K3, K2tog, K9, YO, K3, K4.

Row 10: K4, P4, YO, P9, P2tog, P1, P2tog tbl, P10, YO, P9, K4.

Rep rows 1–10 for patt.

SCARF

CO 45 sts and knit 6 rows.

Work in ocean current patt until piece measures approx 49", ending with row 10.

Knit 6 rows.

BO all sts loosely.

FINISHING

Weave in ends. Block, using the pin-and-mist method (page 76), to smooth and even sts.

SCALLOP Shells

The scallop is probably best known for its beautiful and distinctive shell with radiating ribs, which has inspired artists for centuries. Let the shell inspire you to work this lace-and-wrap-stitch scarf.

FINISHED MEASUREMENTS

Approx 7" x 64"

MATERIALS

3 skeins of Dale of Norway (50% cotton, 40% viscose, 10% silk; 50 g; 114 yds), color 5403 (3)

Size 4 needles or size required to obtain gauge

Cable needle

Stitch holder

GAUGE

29 sts = 4 in scallop shell patt

SCALLOP SHELL PATTERN

(Multiple of 21 + 9)

P4wrap: P4 and sl those sts to cn, wrap yarn counterclockwise around 4 slipped sts 3 times, sl 4 sts back to right-hand needle.

Row 1 (WS): Knit.

Row 2 (RS): K3, purl to last 3 sts, K3.

Row 3: Knit.

Row 4: K4, *YO, K21, rep from * to last 5 sts, K5—53 sts.

Row 5: K3, P3, *(K3, P1) 5 times, P2, rep from * to last 3 sts, K3.

Row 6: K5, *YO, K1, (P3, K1) 5 times, YO, K1, rep from * to last 4 sts, K4—57 sts.

Row 7: K3, *P4, (K3, P1) 5 times, rep from * to last 6 sts, P3, K3.

Row 8: K5, *YO, K1, YO, (ssk, P2) 5 times, (K1, YO) twice, K1, rep from * to last 4 sts, K4—55 sts.

Row 9: K3, *P6, (K2, P1) 5 times, P2, rep from * to last 6 sts, P3, K3.

Row 10: K5, *(YO, K1) 3 times, YO, (ssk, P1) 5 times, (K1, YO) 4 times, K1, rep from * to last 4 sts, K4—61 sts.

Row 11: K3, *P10, (K1, P1) 5 times, P6, rep from * to last 6 sts, P3, K3.

Row 12: K4, *K8, ssk 5 times, K8, rep from * to last 5 sts, K5—51 sts.

Row 13: K3, *P10, P4wrap, P7, rep from * to last 6 sts, P3, K3.

Row 14: Knit.

Rep rows 1–14 for patt.

SCARF

(Make 2 pieces.)

CO 51 sts and work in scallop shell patt until piece measures approx 32", ending with row 14.

Sl all sts to st holder.

Make second piece and leave on needle.

FINISHING

Place sts from holder onto knitting needle. Graft the 2 pieces tog, using kitchener st (page 74). Weave in ends. Block, using the mist method (page 76), to smooth and even sts.

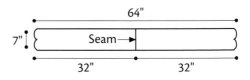

Sea CUCUMBERS

All deep sea divers know that sea cucumbers are not really vegetables and not really a delicacy, but this scarf is pure indulgence. The pattern stitch is an uncomplicated rhythmic pattern of knits and purls that is quickly memorized. The scarf is extra long, allowing the knitter to indulge and enjoy the pattern, and the wearer to indulge by wrapping it around the neck numerous times.

FINISHED MEASUREMENTS

Approx 6" x 98"

MATERIALS

4 skeins of Inca Alpaca from Classic Elite (100% alpaca; 50 g; 100 m/109 yds), color 1109

Size 7 needles or size required to obtain gauge

GAUGE

20 sts = 4" in sea cucumber patt

SEA CUCUMBER PATTERN

(Patt multiple of 8 + 6 plus 8 edge sts)

Row 1 (RS): K4, K4, P2, *K6, P2, rep from * to last 4 sts, K4.

Row 2: K4, P1, K2, *P6, K2, rep from * to last 7 sts, P3, K4.

Row 3: *K6, P2, rep from * to last 6 sts, K6.

Row 4: K4, P3, K2, *P6, K2, rep from * to last 5 sts, P1, K4.

Row 5: K4, P2, *K6, P2, rep from * to last 8 sts, K8.

Row 6: K4, purl to last 4 sts, K4.

Row 7: Knit.

Row 8: K4, purl to last 4 sts, K4.

Rep rows 1–8 for patt.

SCARF

CO 30 sts and knit 7 rows.

Next row: K4, purl to last 4 sts, K4.

Work in sea cucumber patt until piece measures approx 96", ending with row 8.

Knit 7 rows.

BO all sts loosely purlwise.

FINISHING

Weave in ends. Block, using the mist method (page 76), to smooth and even sts.

Design Option: You will have enough yarn for a wider but shorter scarf. CO 46 sts for a finished piece that is 9¼" x 60".

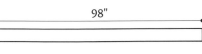

SEA Foam

It's hard to believe this delicate and lacy fabric is made by just knitting. The yarn overs create elongated stitches that add the openwork. This is an easy pattern to try, even if you've never worked lace before.

FINISHED MEASUREMENTS

Approx 14" x 78"

MATERIALS

2 skeins of Gossamer from Karabella Yarns (52% nylon, 30% kid mohair, 18% polyester; 50 g/1.78 oz; 200 m/222 yds), color 6105 Ice Blue

Size 9 needles or size required to obtain gauge

GAUGE

13 sts = 4" in sea foam patt

SEA FOAM PATTERN

(Multiple of 10 + 4)

Row 1 (RS): Knit.

Row 2: Knit.

Row 3: K10, *YO twice, K1, YO 3 times, K1, YO 4 times, K1, YO 3 times, K1, YO twice, K6, rep from * to last 4 sts, K4.

Row 4: Knit across, dropping all YOs off needle.

Rows 5 and 6: Knit.

Row 7: K5, *YO twice, K1, YO 3 times, K1, YO 4 times, K1, YO 3 times, K1, YO twice, K6, rep from *, end last repeat with K5 instead of K6.

Row 8: Knit across, dropping all YOs off needle.

Rep rows 1–8 for patt.

SCARF

CO 44 sts and knit 2 rows.

Work in sea foam patt until piece measures approx 77½", ending with row 8.

Knit 4 rows.

BO all sts loosely.

FINISHING

Weave in all ends. Block, using the wet method (page 76), to smooth and even sts. You may have to use your hands to extend elongated sts as you pin in place.

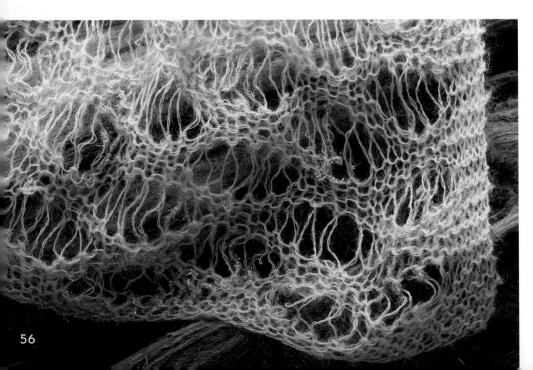

SEA Horses

The sea horse is actually a fish with a horse-shaped head. Its colors are variable but this scarf portrays red sea horses, made with a cable stitch, hiding in coral lace. The entire piece is edged in a picot crochet stitch that is easy to work.

FINISHED MEASUREMENTS

Approx 14" x 64" (including crochet edge)

MATERIALS

8 skeins of Cotton Twist from Berroco (70% cotton, 30% rayon; 50 g/1.75 oz; 78 m/85 yds), color 8311 ⓸

Size 9 circular (36") needle or size required to obtain gauge

Size 10½ needles for bind off

Cable needle

Size I-9 (5.5 mm) crochet hook

GAUGE

13 sts = 4" in sea horse patt on size 9 needles after blocking

SEA HORSE PATTERN

(Patt multiple of 8 plus 4 edge sts)

Row 1 (RS): K2, *K4, YO, K2tog, YO, K2tog, * rep from * to last 2 sts, K2.

Row 2 and all WS rows: K2, purl to last 2 sts, K2.

Row 3: K2, *K4, YO, K2tog, YO, K2tog, rep from * to last 2 sts, K2.

Row 5: K2, *sl 2 to cn and hold at front, K2, K2 from cn, YO, K2tog, YO, K2tog, rep from * to last 2 sts, K2.

Row 7: K2, *K4, YO, K2tog, YO, K2tog, rep from * to last 2 sts, K2.

Row 9: K2, *YO, K2tog, YO, K2tog, K4, rep from * to last 2 sts, K2.

Row 11: K2, *YO, K2tog, YO, K2tog, K4, rep from * to last 2 sts, K2.

Row 13: K2, *YO, K2tog, YO, K2tog, sl 2 to cn and hold at back, K2, K2 from cn, rep from * to last 2 sts, K2.

Row 15: K2, *YO, K2tog, YO, K2tog, K4, rep from * to last 2 sts, K2.

Row 16: K2, purl to last 2 sts, K2.

Rep rows 1–16 for patt.

SCARF

Using cable cast on (see page 60), loosely CO 204 sts. Knit 1 row.

Work a total of 6 sea horse patt reps.

Knit 1 row.

With size 10½ needles, loosely BO all sts purlwise.

Cable cast on: Make a slipknot and place on needle. Knit into stitch and place resulting stitch on left needle by inserting left needle into stitch from right side of loop. *Insert right needle between two stitches, wrap yarn around needle, pull new loop through to front, and place on left needle. Repeat from * for specified number of stitches.

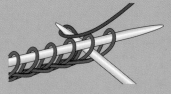

Insert needle between two stitches. Knit a stitch.

Place new stitch on left needle.

PICOT CROCHET EDGE

Row 1: Sc around all edges, working 3 sc in corner sts.

Row 2: Ch 1, work 2 sc in each of next 2 sc, *ch 4, sl st in first ch of ch 4 (picot made), sc in each of next 3 sc, rep from * to last st, work 2 sc in last st, join with sl st. Fasten off.

FINISHING

Weave in ends. Block, using the pin-and-mist method (page 76), to smooth and even sts.

64"

14"

Measurements include crochet edge.

SNAILS

The whorled shell of the snail is an engineering masterpiece, and as you work this lace pattern, you will be creating your own work of art. Each snail, with its beautiful coiled shell and antennae stretched high, emerges one right after the next.

FINISHED MEASUREMENTS

Approx 5" x 50"

MATERIALS

3 skeins of Glacé from Berroco (100% rayon; 50 g/1.75 oz; 69 m/75 yds), color 2657 ④

Size 7 needles or size required to obtain gauge

Tapestry needle

GAUGE

15 sts = 4" in snail patt after blocking

SNAIL PATTERN

The "YO twice" is worked as 2 sts on the subsequent row.

Row 1 (WS): K5, P1, YO, P2tog, K8, YO, K2tog, K1.

Row 2 (RS): K3, YO, K2tog, K5, K2tog, YO, K1, YO, ssk, K2, YO twice, K2—21 sts.

Row 3: K3, P1, K1, P2tog tbl, YO, P3, YO, P2tog, K6, YO, K2tog, K1.

Row 4: K3, YO, K2tog, K3, K2tog, YO, K2, K2tog, YO, K1, YO, ssk, K2, YO twice, K2—23 sts.

Row 5: K3, P1, K1, P2tog tbl, YO, P3, YO, P2tog, P2, YO, P2tog, K4, YO, K2tog, K1.

Row 6: K3, YO, K2tog, K1, (K2tog, YO, K2) twice, YO, ssk, K1, YO, ssk, K2, YO twice, K2—25 sts.

Row 7: K3, P1, K1, (P2tog tbl, YO, P1) twice, YO, P2tog, P1, YO, P2tog, P2, YO, P2tog, K2, YO, K2tog, K1.

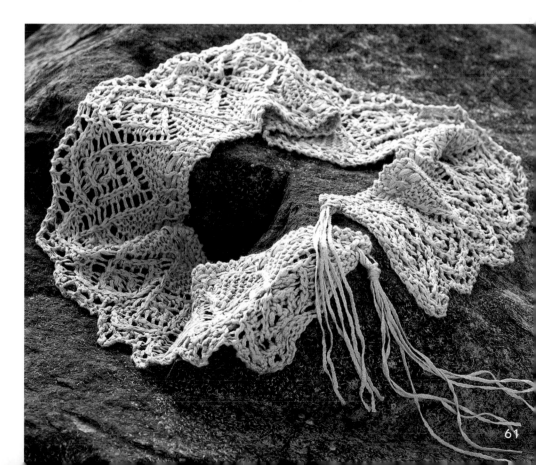

Row 8: K3, YO, K3tog, YO, K2, K2tog, YO, K1, K2tog, YO, K3, YO, ssk, K1, YO, ssk, K2tog, YO twice, K2tog.

Row 9: K2, P1, K1, P2, YO, P2tog, P1, YO, P3tog, YO, P1, P2tog tbl, YO, P2, P2tog tbl, YO, K3, YO, K2tog, K1.

Row 10: K3, YO, K2tog, (K2, YO, ssk) twice, K3, K2tog, YO, K2, sl 1, K2tog, psso, YO twice, K2tog—24 sts.

Row 11: K2, P5, YO, P2tog, P1, P2tog tbl, YO, P2, P2tog tbl, YO, K5, YO, K2tog, K1.

Row 12: K3, YO, K2tog, K4, YO, ssk, K2, YO, K3tog, YO, K2, K3tog, YO, K2tog, K1—22 sts.

Row 13: K3, P1, K3, YO, P2tog, P1, P2tog tbl, YO, K7, YO, K2tog, K1.

Row 14: K3, YO, K2tog, K6, YO, K3tog, YO, K2, K3tog, YO, K3tog—19 sts.

Rep rows 1–14 for patt.

SCARF

CO 19 sts and knit 1 row.

Work in snail patt until piece measures approx 50", ending with row 14.

Knit 1 row.

BO all sts loosely.

FINISHING

Weave in ends. Block, using the pin-and-mist method (page 76), to smooth and even sts.

Woven edging: Cut 6 strands of yarn, each 70" long. With RS facing you and tapestry needle threaded with 3 strands of yarn, weave over and under eyelets along straight edge. Rep with another 3 strands in second set of eyelets. Secure ends with overhand knot (page 19).

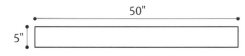

STARFISH on the BEACH

Typically starfish have five arms, but some may have more or less. This lacy starfish is surrounded by seed stitch. A slit allows the scarf to be secured around the neck.

FINISHED MEASUREMENTS

Approx 6" x 45"

MATERIALS

2 skeins of Synchronicity from Alchemy Yarns (50% silk, 50% wool; 50 g; 118 yds), color 1783 Topaz ⟨4⟩

Size 8 needles or size required to obtain gauge

GAUGE

21 sts = 4" in starfish lace patt

SEED STITCH

(Even number of sts)

Row 1 (RS): *K1, P1, rep from *.

Row 2: *P1, K1, rep from *. (Knit the purl sts and purl the knit sts as they face you.)

STARFISH LACE PATTERN

(Worked over 32 sts)

Row 1 (RS): (K1, P1) twice, knit to last 4 sts, (K1, P1) twice.

Row 2 and all WS rows: (P1, K1) twice, purl to last 4 sts, (P1, K1) twice.

Row 3: (K1, P1) twice, K5, K2tog, YO, K1 tbl, YO, K2tog, K5, K2tog, YO, K1 tbl, YO, K2tog, K4, (K1, P1) twice.

Row 5: (K1, P1) twice, K6, K2tog, YO, K1 tbl, YO, K2tog, K3, K2tog, YO, K1 tbl, YO, K2tog, K5, (K1, P1) twice.

Row 7: K1, P1) twice, K7, K2tog, YO, K1 tbl, YO, K2tog, K1, K2tog, YO, K1 tbl, YO, K2tog, K6, (K1, P1) twice.

Row 9: (K1, P1) twice, K8, K2tog, YO, K1 tbl, YO, sl 1, K2tog, psso, YO, K1 tbl, YO, K2tog, K7, (K1, P1) twice.

Row 11: (K1, P1) twice, K10, YO, sl 1, K2tog, psso, YO, K2tog, YO, K9, (K1, P1) twice.

Row 13: (K1, P1) twice , K5, sl 1, K2tog, psso, (YO, K1 tbl) twice, YO, K2tog, YO, sl 1, K2tog, psso, (YO, K1 tbl) twice, YO, sl 1, K2tog, psso, K4, (K1, P1) twice.

Row 15: (K1, P1) twice, K4, sl 1, K2tog, psso, (YO, K1 tbl) twice, YO, K2tog, YO, sl 1, K2tog, psso, YO, K2tog, (YO, K1 tbl) twice, YO, sl 1, K2tog, psso, K3, (K1, P1) twice.

Rows 17 and 19: (K1, P1) twice, K10, K2tog, YO, K1 tbl, YO, K2tog, K9, (K1, P1) twice.

Row 21: (K1, P1) twice, K11, K2tog, YO, K1 tbl, K10, (K1, P1) twice.

Row 23: (K1, P1) twice, knit to last 4 sts, (K1, P1) twice.

Row 24: (P1, K1) twice, purl to last 4 sts, (P1, K1) twice.

Rep rows 1–24 for patt.

SCARF

CO 32 sts and work in seed st for 2", ending with WS row.

Make slit:

Row 1 (RS): Work 11 seed sts, BO center 10 sts, work 11 seed sts.

Row 2: Work 11 seed sts, CO 10 sts with backward loop (see "Backward loop" at right), work 11 seed sts.

Work 4 rows in seed st.

Beg starfish lace patt and work until piece measures approx 42", ending with row 24.

Work in seed st until piece measures 45".

BO all sts in patt loosely.

FINISHING

Weave in ends. Block, using the mist method (page 76), to smooth and even sts.

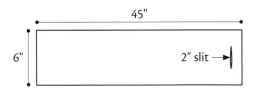

Backward loop: This is an easy cast on whenever you need to add stitches within a row. *Form loop so end of yarn is in front of needle. Insert right needle into this loop and tighten gently. Repeat from * for desired number of stitches.

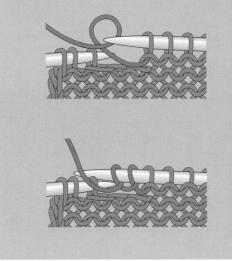

SURF'S Up

Rather than search the world for that ideal wave, create your own perfect waves. These waves may look complicated, but with the slip-stitch technique, you are using only one color at a time in the row.

FINISHED MEASUREMENTS

Approx 7" x 65" (including crochet edge)

MATERIALS

Calmer from Rowan Yarns (75% cotton, 25% acrylic; 50 g; 160 m, 175 yds) in the following colors: (4)

A (dark) 2 skeins color 479 Slosh

B (light) 1 skein   color 475 Tinkerbell

Size 10 needles or size required to obtain gauge

Size J-10 (6 mm) crochet hook

GAUGE

21 sts = 4" in slip-stitch wave patt

SLIP-STITCH WAVE PATTERN

(Multiple of 5 + 2)

Do not cut yarn when changing colors; carry unused yarn loosely up side of work.

On RS rows, sl all sts wyib. On WS rows, sl all sts wyif.

Row 1 (RS): With B, K5, *sl 1, K4, rep from * to last 2 sts, sl 1, K1.

Row 2 and all B WS rows: Knit the knit sts on previous row, sl the sl sts on previous row.

Row 3: With A, K1, *sl 1, K4, rep from * to last st, K1.

Row 4 and all A WS rows: Purl the knit sts on previous row, sl the sl sts on previous row.

Row 5: With B, K2, *sl 1, K4, rep from *.

Row 7: With A, K3, *sl 1, K4, rep from * to last 4 sts, sl 1, K3.

Row 9: With B, *K4, sl 1, rep from * to last 2 sts, K2.

Row 11: With A, K5, *sl 1, K4, rep from * to last 2 sts, sl 1, K1.

Row 13: With B, K1, *sl 1, K4, rep from * to last st, K1.

Row 15: With A, K2, *sl 1, K4, rep from *.

Row 17: With B, K3, *sl 1, K4, rep from * to last 4 sts, sl 1, K3.

Row 19: With A, K2, *sl 1, K4, rep from *.

Row 21: With B, K1, *sl 1, K4, rep from * to last st, K1.

Row 23: With A, K5, *sl 1, K4, rep from * to last 2 sts, sl 1, K1.

Row 25: With B, *K4, sl 1, rep from * to last 2 sts, K2.

Row 27: With A, K3, *sl 1, K4, rep from * to last 4 sts, sl 1, K3.

Row 29: With B, K2, *sl 1, K4, rep from *.

Row 31: With A, K1, *sl 1, K4, rep from * to last st, K1.

Row 32: Rep row 4.

Rep rows for 1–32 for patt.

SCARF

With A, CO 32 sts and knit 1 row.

Change to B and work slip-stitch wave patt until piece measures approx 64", ending with row 32.

With A, knit 1 row.

Loosely BO all sts purlwise.

FINISHING

With A, RS facing you, and J crochet hook, sc around entire scarf, working 3 sc in each corner. Sc 1 more rnd, working 3 sc in each corner st. Work 1 rnd of crab st (page 75). Weave in all ends. Block, using the damp-towel method (page 76), to smooth and even sts.

65"

7"

Measurements include crochet edge.

TURTLE Tracks

Travel on shore is awkward for turtles, and they leave a very distinctive track in the sand. This turtle-track pattern is edged with vertical garter-stitch scallops and delicately knotted fringe.

FINISHED MEASUREMENTS

Approx 13" to 15" x 66" (without fringe)

MATERIALS

6 skeins of Dune from Trendsetter Yarns (36% mohair, 35% cotton, 15% nylon, 12% acrylic, 2% metal; 50 g; 82 yds), color 115 (5)

Size 10½ needles or size required to obtain gauge

Size I-9 (5.5 mm) crochet hook

GAUGE

12 sts = 4" in turtle tracks patt

TURTLE TRACKS PATTERN WITH SCALLOPED EDGE

(Worked over 41 sts)

Row 1 (WS): K1, K1f&b, K5, P6, K3, P9, K3, P6, K5, K1f&b, K1—43 sts.

Row 2 (RS): K1, K1f&b, K12, P3, YO, K4, ssk, K3, P3, K12, K1f&b, K1—45 sts.

Row 3: K1, K1f&b, K7, P6, K3, P9, K3, P6, K7, K1f&b, K1—47 sts.

Row 4: K1, K1f&b, K14, P3, K1, YO, K4, ssk, K2, P3, K14, K1f&b, K1—49 sts.

Row 5: K1, K1f&b, K9, P6, K3, P9, K3, P6, K9, K1f&b, K1—51 sts.

Row 6: K1, K1f&b, K16, P3, K2, YO, K4, ssk, K1, P3, K16, K1f&b, K1—53 sts.

Row 7: K1, K1f&b, K11, P6, K3, P9, K3, P6, K11, K1f&b, K1—55 sts.

Row 8: K1, K1f&b, K18, P3, K3, YO, K4, ssk, P3, K18, K1f&b, K1—57 sts.

Row 9: K1, ssk, K12, P6, K3, P9, K3, P6, K12, K2tog, K1—55 sts.

Row 10: K1, ssk, K17, P3, K3, K2tog, K4, YO, P3, K17, K2tog, K1—53 sts.

Row 11: K1, ssk, K10, P6, K3, P9, K3, P6, K10, K2tog, K1—51 sts.

Row 12: K1, ssk, K15, P3, K2, K2tog, K4, YO, K1, P3, K15, K2tog, K1—49 sts.

Row 13: K1, ssk, K8, P6, K3, P9, K3, P6, K8, K2tog, K1—47 sts.

Row 14: K1, ssk, K13, P3, K1, K2tog, K4, YO, K2, P3, K13, K2tog, K1—45 sts.

Row 15: K1, ssk, K6, P6, K3, P9, K3, P6, K6, K2tog, K1—43 sts.

Row 16: K1, ssk, K11, P3, K2tog, K4, YO, K3, P3, K11, K2tog, K1—41 sts.

Rep rows 1–16 for patt.

SCARF

CO 41 sts and knit 1 row.

Work in turtle tracks patt until piece measures approx 66", ending with row 1.

Knit 1 row.

BO all sts loosely.

FINISHING

Weave in ends. Block, using the mist method (page 76), to smooth and even sts.

Fringe: Cut 16 strands of yarn, each 24" long. Using crochet hook, attach 8 single strands of fringe (page 74) along each bottom edge as shown at right. Using overhand knot (page 19), make 2 rows of knots as shown in diagram.

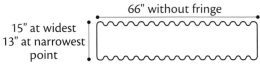

66" without fringe

15" at widest
13" at narrowest point

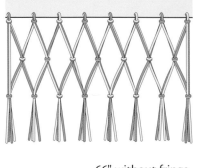

Abbreviations AND Glossary

approx	approximately
beg	begin(ning)
BO	bind off
ch	chain
cn	cable needle
CO	cast on
cont	continue
dc	double crochet
dec	decrease
g	grams
inc	increase
K1f&b	knit into front and back of same stitch—1 stitch increased
K	knit
K2tog	knit 2 sts together—1 stitch decreased
K3tog	knit 3 stitches together—2 stitches decreased
M1	make 1 stitch: Insert the left needle from front to back under strand between last stitch worked and next stitch on left needle. Knit this lifted strand through the back loop—1 stitch increased.
m	meter
oz	ounces
P	purl
P2tog	purl 2 stitches together—1 stitch decreased
P3tog	purl 3 stitches together—2 stitches decreased
patt	pattern

pm	place marker
psso	pass slipped stitch over
p2sso	pass 2 slipped stitches over
PU	pick up and knit
rem	remain(s)(ing)
rep(s)	repeat(s)
RS	right side
sc	single crochet
sk	skip
sl	slip
sl st	slip stitch: slip 1 stitch purlwise with yarn in back unless otherwise instructed
sl 1, K2tog, psso	slip 1 stitch as if to knit, knit 2 stitches together, pass slipped stitch over—2 stitches decreased
sl 2, K1, p2sso	slip 2 stitches together as if to knit, knit 1 stitch, pass 2 slipped stitches over—2 stitches decreased
ssk	slip, slip, knit: Slip 2 stitches separately as if to knit. Insert left needle into these 2 stitches from left to right and knit them together through the back loops—1 stitch decreased.
st(s)	stitch(es)
tbl	through back loop
tog	together
WS	wrong side
wyib	with yarn in back
wyif	with yarn in front
yds	yards
YO	yarn over

TECHNIQUES

Following are a few of the techniques used in this book.

Fringe: Cut fringe to the specified length. Fold fringe in half. Insert crochet hook from front to back of work. Catch the folded fringe and pull through the knitted piece, creating a loop. Draw fringe ends through the loop and pull to tighten. Trim as necessary to even lengths.

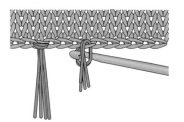

Joining a new ball of yarn: Whenever possible, attach a new ball of yarn at the beginning of the row. Tie the new strand onto the old tail with a single knot. Slide the new knot up the old tail to the needle and begin knitting with the new yarn. Weave in the tails when you finish the project.

Kitchener stitch: Place the stitches to be grafted onto two needles and fasten off the working yarn. Thread a tapestry needle with a length of yarn approximately three times the width of the seam. Hold the two knitting needles together in the left hand with the points facing to the right and the wrong sides of the knitting facing together. Hold the threaded tapestry needle in the right hand.

1. Go through the first stitch on the front needle as if to purl and leave it on the needle. Go through the first stitch on the back needle as if to knit and leave it on the needle.

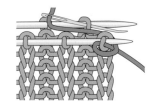

2. Go through the first stitch on the front needle as if to knit and slip it off the needle. Go through the second stitch on the front needle as if to purl and leave it on the needle.

3. Go through the first stitch on the back needle as if to purl and slip it off the needle. Go through the second stitch on the back needle as if to knit and leave it on the needle.

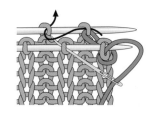

Here's a shortcut to help you remember what to do:

Front needle: Knit off, purl on.

Back needle: Purl off, knit on.

Repeat steps 2 and 3 until all stitches are joined, adjusting tension to match tension of knitted work.

Yarn over (YO): If the last stitch worked is a knit stitch, bring the yarn between the two needles to the front. Take the yarn over the right-hand needle to the back: one yarn over made. If the last stitch worked is a purl stitch, the yarn is already in the front. Take the yarn over the right needle to the back: one yarn over made. After the yarn over, if the next stitch to be worked is a knit stitch, the yarn is already in position to work. If the next stitch to be worked is a purl st, bring the yarn between the needles to the front. For multiple yarn overs, repeat for the desired number of yarn overs.

Knit in row below: Knit into the center of the stitch below the next stitch on the left needle and drop the stitch above off the left needle.

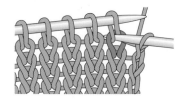

CROCHET

Chain (ch): Wrap yarn around hook and pull through loop on hook.

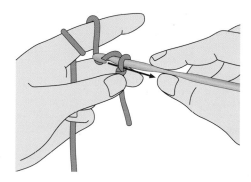

Crab stitch (or reverse single crochet): Work a row of single crochet along edge with right side facing you. At the end of the row, *do not turn work*. Work a row of crab stitch from left to right. Insert hook into first stitch to the right, yarn over hook, and pull through both loops on hook. Repeat around; join and fasten off.

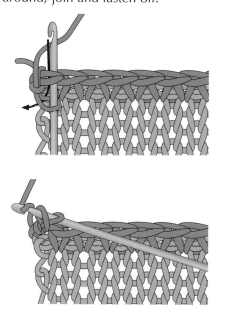

Double crochet (dc): Working from right to left with right side facing you, yarn over hook, insert hook into next stitch, yarn over hook, and pull loop to front (three loops on hook). Yarn over hook and pull through first two loops on hook (two loops remain on hook). Yarn over hook and pull through remaining two loops (one loop remains on hook).

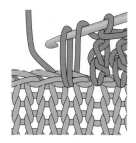

Yarn over hook, insert hook into stitch, yarn over hook, pull through to front.

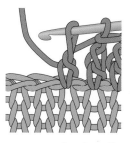

Yarn over hook, pull through two loops on hook.

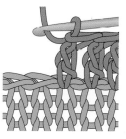

Yarn over hook, pull through remaining two loops on hook.

Single crochet (sc): Working from right to left with right side facing you, insert the hook into next stitch, yarn over hook, pull loop to front, yarn over hook, and pull loop through both loops on hook. Space stitches so the edge lies flat.

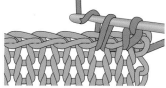

Insert hook into stitch, yarn over hook, pull loop through to front, yarn over hook.

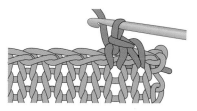

Pull loop through both loops on hook.

The formula for spacing stitches on a vertical edge is to work into each knot at the edge. For a horizontal row, the formula is every one and one-half stitches. However, even using the formulas as a guide, it may be necessary to skip or add stitches to keep the edge flat.

When working a crochet edge on a knitted piece, always begin by working a row of single crochet to stabilize the edges. To work additional rows of single crochet, insert the hook under both loops of the stitch below, and then work one single crochet into each stitch in the previous row.

75

Slip stitch (sl st): Working from right to left with right side facing you, insert hook into next stitch, yarn over hook, pull loop through stitch, and in one continuous motion, draw it through the loop on the hook.

Insert hook into stitch, yarn over hook.

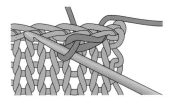

Pull loop of yarn through stitch and loop on hook.

BLOCKING

First choose a flat waterproof surface to spread out the piece to be blocked. You can purchase blocking boards for this purpose. The top on an ironing board works well for smaller pieces, or the floor covered with a towel also works. Regardless of the method used for blocking, the piece should remain in place until dry.

Damp-towel method: Lay the knitted piece on the surface, shaping to specified dimensions. Dampen a towel, large enough to cover the knitted piece; running a saturated towel through the spin cycle of the washing machine works well. Place the damp towel over the knitted piece for 1 to 2 hours. Remove the towel, but leave the piece to dry completely before moving.

Mist method: Lay the knitted piece on the surface, shaping to specified dimensions. Fill a clean spray bottle with water and mist the piece lightly with water. Allow to dry completely before moving.

Pin-and-mist method: Lay the knitted piece on the surface and pin to specified measurements. Fill a clean spray bottle with water and mist the piece heavily with water. Allow to dry completely before removing pins.

Wet-blocking method: Dip knitted piece in cool water. Gently squeeze out the water. Do not wring or twist the piece. Roll the piece in an absorbent bath towel to blot out the excess water. Spread the piece on the surface and pin to specified dimensions. Allow to dry completely before removing pins.

RESOURCES

For a list of shops in your area that carry the yarns mentioned in this book, contact the following companies:

Alchemy Yarns of Transformation
www.alchemyyarns.com
Synchronicity

Art Yarns
www.artyarns.com
Regal Silk
Silk Rhapsody

Berroco Yarns
www.berroco.com
Cotton Twist
Glacé
Ultra Alpaca
Zen

Blue Heron Yarns
www.blueheronyarns.com
Cotton Woven Ribbon

Cascade Yarns
www.cascadeyarns.com
Cascade 220

Classic Elite Yarns
www.classiceliteyarns.com
Classic Silk
Inca Alpaca
Premiere

Cricket Cove
www.cricketcove.com
Qiviut

Dale of Norway
www.daleyarns.com
Svale

Hanah Silk
www.artemisinc.com
Hanah Silk Ribbon

Harrisville Designs
www.harrisville.com
New England Shetland

Judi and Company
www.judiandco.com
Stardust

Karabella Yarns
www.karabellayarns.com
Gossamer

Knit One Crochet Too
www.knitonecrochettoo.com
Douceur et Soie

Koigu Wood Design
www.koigu.com
KPPPM

Muench Yarns
www.muenchyarns.com
String of Pearls

Rowan Yarns
Westminster Fibers
email: wfibers@aol.com
Calmer

South West Trading Company
www.soysilk.com
Bamboo

Trendsetter Yarns
www.trendsetteryarns.com
Dune

Wool in the Woods
www.woolinthewoods.com
Cherub

KNITTING AND CROCHET TITLES

Martingale®
& COMPANY

America's Best-Loved Craft & Hobby Books®
America's Best-Loved Knitting Books®

CROCHET

Creative Crochet

Crochet for Babies
and Toddlers

Crochet for Tots

Crochet from the Heart

Crocheted Pursenalities—*New!*

Crocheted Socks!

Cute Crochet for Kids

The Essential Book of
Crochet Techniques

Eye-Catching Crochet

First Crochet

Fun and Funky Crochet

Funky Chunky
Crocheted Accessories

**The Little Box of Crochet
for Baby—*New!***

The Little Box of
Crocheted Bags

The Little Box of Crocheted Hats
and Scarves

The Little Box of Crocheted
Ponchos and Wraps

**The Little Box of Crocheted
Scarves—*New!***

More Crocheted
Aran Sweaters

KNITTING

200 Knitted Blocks

365 Knitting Stitches a Year:
Perpetual Calendar

A to Z of Knitting—*New!*

Big Knitting

Blankets, Hats, and Booties

Double Exposure

Everyday Style

Fair Isle Sweaters Simplified

First Knits

Fun and Funky Knitting

Funky Chunky
Knitted Accessories

Handknit Style

Handknit Style II

Knits, Knots, Buttons,
and Bows

Knitted Shawls, Stoles,
and Scarves

The Knitter's Book of
Finishing Techniques

**Knitting Beyond the Basics—
*New!***

Knitting with Gigi—*New!*

Lavish Lace

The Little Box of Knits
for Baby

The Little Box of Knitted
Ponchos and Wraps

The Little Box of
Knitted Throws

The Little Box of Scarves

The Little Box of Scarves II

Modern Classics

More Sensational Knitted Socks—*New!*

The Pleasures of Knitting

Pursenalities

Pursenality Plus

Ribbon Style

Romantic Style

Sarah Dallas Knitting

Saturday Sweaters

Sensational Knitted Socks

Silk Knits

Simply Beautiful Sweaters

**Special Little Knits from
Just One Skein—*New!***

Top Down Sweaters—*New!*

The Ultimate Knitted Tee

Wrapped in Comfort—*New!*

The Yarn Stash Workbook

Our books are available at bookstores and your favorite craft, fabric, and yarn retailers.
If you don't see the title you're looking for, visit us at **www.martingale-pub.com** or contact us at:

1-800-426-3126

International: 1-425-483-3313 • Fax: 1-425-486-7596 • Email: info@martingale-pub.com

3/07 Knit